AF580496

YOU COULD'VE SAID NO

SELF-LOVING DECISIONS ENHANCE
YOUR QUALITY OF LIFE

CAROLE ALTMAN, Ph.D.

Carole's other books:

"You Can Be Your Own Sex Therapist"

"A 101 Ways to Make Love Happen"

"From the Files of a Sex Therapist"

"Don't Have Sex Again Until You Have Read This Book"

Copyright © 2020 Carole Altman, Ph.D.

All rights reserved.

ISBN: 9798669500061

DEDICATION

I dedicate ***"YOU COULD'VE SAID NO"*** to my daughter JODI LYNN AMORUSO. Jodi was always at my side encouraging me to stand tall, be confident and speak my mind. She especially endorsed boundaries, truth and my ability to know when to say ***NO.*** Jodi's children, Robert and Alyssa, are continuing the support and encouragement. They actually applaud, even if I say ***NO*** to an idea of theirs. The path I follow is influenced by their love and validation.

This book is a tribute to the real-life characters in these stories, my dearest friends and protective, caring family.

Writing this book with my husband, Milton Zaslowsky at my side has been a joyous experience. His encouragement, kindness and love constantly motivates me.

He is my LION AT THE GATE.

TABLE OF CONTENTS

ACKNOWLEDGMENTS

Nothing is ever created or built by one person. Everything worthwhile is a collaboration of the minds and souls of many.

"You Could've Said NO" is not an exception. It is a creation of my dearest friends, my muses, editors and emotional support. Thank you to all who held my hand, encouraged me, generously shared their skills, talents, unmatched intelligence and lots of love.

Camille Duskin was always by my side, advising, motivating and sharing fun and love. Kathleen Pasieka quietly and effectively made it happen with a touch, a word and an idea. Michele's ever-present smile, kindness and actions, spurred me on. Rictor Riolo is the genius behind the cover, the design and the publication of this book. Rictor is an indispensable added value and I am totally indebted and thankful.

Milton Zaslowsky earns mention and gratitude, guaranteeing a quiet environment, preparing food and doing chores enabling me to concentrate. Thank you for your love, endless attention and lots of kudos.

Thank you to the men and women who shared their triumphs and their tragedies. Hopefully they effectively and powerfully helped others to avoid the pain and suffering which are the results of not saying ***NO***.

Love,
Carole Altman

"Loving yourself is your survival kit."

– Carole Altman

INTRODUCTION

"YOU COULD'VE SAID NO" is a book you will treasure. It is a book born of necessity. Too many of us cause ourselves pain and suffering because we agree to destructive requests. This collection of lessons in the art of survival offers solutions. These real-life stories clearly show the challenges we face. In every situation there is a moment of truth: a moment in which a decision is necessary. It is at this precise moment that your decision must be positive for yourself. You are the captain of your life. Be in control and always protect yourself. Ask yourself, ***"What is best for me at this moment?"*** If you don't determine what is best for you, the results can be catastrophic.

"YOU COULD'VE SAID NO" details the reality which plays out in too many lives. These are stories of men and women faced with the most impactful decisions of their lives. Some end with successful outcomes. Others, less fortunate, end in defeat. This book gives you a step-by-step program of effective techniques and procedures which will prevent destructive decisions. Reading ***"YOU COULD'VE SAID NO"*** will bring you the necessary truths which are often too painful to accept.

You will be shocked at the destruction and pain suffered as a result of wrong decisions. It is imperative that you recognize your motivation when making a decision. You may be rationalizing and denying truths to avoid saying ***NO.*** The skills necessary for good decisions are here. This is a step-by-step path to a positive, self-protective life of choices. You will find these effective tools are of infinite value as you make protective decisions and assert yourself. Gaining respect and loyalty will be a precious bonus when you take charge and demand positive results. This is your roadmap to survival regardless of the circumstances or difficulties. It is a clear and simple path to success every time you're faced with a major decision.

This book is truly an essential guideline to stave off catastrophes. This information is your ammunition to avoid incomprehensible loss. Stories of major mistakes are heartbreaking. Walk in the shoes of these men and women. Feel their pain. Recognize their mistakes so you will ***NOT*** be a victim. Your decisions will be protective and satisfying. Take the path of self-protective choices and travel in your chosen direction. Protecting and honoring your own needs is your mantra. Send the message of confidence and love and journey towards emotional success.

"YOU COULD'VE SAID NO" is a roadmap to good decision-making. You will NEVER again be mistreated, misled or dismissed. These simple, effective and easy-to-follow ideas will be lifesaving in many situations. Decisions require concentration, objectivity and self-confidence. These step-by-step ideas will enable you to avoid destructive decisions.

You will read specific and necessary questions that you need to ask before making any decision. The questions you MUST ask and the information you MUST be given become the foundation of your decision. Making constructive decisions will be easy. The benefits of loving and protecting yourself result in feelings of self-confidence and pride.

"YOU COULD'VE SAID NO" is a book replete with infinite personal benefits. It is a book which will save you from untold misfortune. It is a collection of lessons in survival and love. It is a book of knowledge which protects, strengthens and encourages.

Many issues require you to make a decision. You must be protective of your own power to decide in your favor. You must be aware of being self-protective. Be especially careful when you are asked for something ***they*** need. Your needs are not considered. Sadly, you will learn that trust is not implied in every situation. Whether this involves a relative or friend, we must always be aware that there may be negative aspects to any situation.

Check your trust barometer. Are you suspicious and inquisitive? Do you rely on emotion? You may have had positive experiences with friends or family members in the past. These experiences should not be a deciding factor in your decisions now. Trust is not consistent. It flows with emotions and needs. Each decision is crucial and contains multiple ramifications. A son or daughter, a relative or friend, is not necessarily on YOUR side. They are not necessarily against you, but too often they are decidedly for themselves.

For example DON'T assume that those close to you are always considering YOUR needs. You will learn to discover and investigate the facts before making any decision. YOU are in charge of YOUR NEEDS. YOU must look out for YOU. Realizing this is a necessary truth will ensure that your life will be smoother and your actions will be in YOUR favor. Each decision you make will be determined by your needs and your health. ***Remember the mantra, what is best for me at this moment?*** Being strong, assertive and self-protective will earn you respect and admiration.

This book details many of the scurrilous behaviors of our loved ones. You may be blinded by the relationship or by the love and trust you have in others. This book details all of the angles, the gyrations and the selfish and insensitive demands. The real-life stories are replete with warning signals that will burn into your brain, forever flashing, a red bullseye. The pain inflicted by a loved one is difficult to grasp or to believe. This is a book of warning signals and avoidance techniques which will be of continuing value to you. Life is full of challenges. ***NO*** is a necessary tool in your survival box. When you recognize the ***need*** to reject a request, you take charge of your life and face challenges successfully. You will learn to take your time before making any decisions and think about the consequences of your decision. You will recognize the need for information. Knowing the facts will give you the security of deciding in your own favor. You will benefit from the power of ***NO***.

These stories are heartbreaking. You may be infuriated as you read the intense pain perpetuated in the name of love. You will be shocked by the manipulation and destruction of relationships suffered at the hands of their own flesh and blood. The building blocks of your confidence can be weakened and even destroyed if you allow it. The information on these pages offers the knowledge and strength for you to avoid any destruction. You are a witness to the pain of the victims. With this information, you will avoid these or any similar mistakes. You are now informed and equipped with all the skills you need to make good decisions. You will NOT make the mistakes of the men and women who did not say ***NO.***

You will also learn how alternative behaviors triumph. Determination and fortitude are the walls which protect us. You will own the keys to maintaining independence, achieving your goals and avoiding the pitfalls. Becoming self-assured and protective is an absolute necessity. Utilizing techniques and ideas in this book guarantees successful results. If ***NO*** is the appropriate answer it will be without any self-retaliation or fear. If ***YES*** is the right answer, it will be made with confidence and self-protection.

During the Coronavirus quarantine of 2020, I wrote daily messages in my "pandemic diary." I have included some of them because they relate to the messages in this book.

This book actually defines the factors which are essential to making positive decisions. I know that attitude is a powerful influence on our behavior. Attitude is our defining umbrella as we go forward in life. It is a scientific fact that attitude is the guiding influence which prescribes who we are and what we do. Therefore, being aware of your attitude about issues ought to be an important factor when faced with any serious decision.

PANDEMIC DIARY
Day 18
March 30, 2020

ATTITUDE

The word of the day is ATTITUDE. With a loving attitude, we will feel the closeness, the cooperation and the positivity. Recognizing your own attitude helps you to appreciate how influential it is.

"Attitude is a little thing, which makes a big difference." – Winston Churchill

You choose your attitude every day. The choice you make makes a big difference in everything you do. You meet a friend for lunch and say, "Wow, this place looks great." Or you say, "Let's get out of here. It's lousy looking."

You have a pain in your back and continually

complain or you don't even mention it. You like your husband's shirt, but say nothing; or you praise the way he looks. Your friend brings you a gift, and you smile in appreciation. Or, you tell her thanks, you have one just like it.

These are choices of ATTITUDE. You're kind, positive, encouraging and supportive. Alternatively, your ATTITUDE is negative. It's essential that you know what your attitude is and learn to control it if necessary. If you have a flat tire, you have to change it. Just do it. Choose happiness and friendship by choosing to see the world through rose-colored glasses.

Your ATTITUDE actually speaks volumes the moment you enter a room. Are you seen as positive? Do you appear to be confident? Are you very unhappy and choose to share that negativity with others? Are you excited to be alive? It is all out there as clearly as though you're carrying a sign describing your ATTITUDE.

You can actually determine your lifestyle, your accomplishments, your feelings and your behaviors by choosing the most positive of ATTITUDES. There is an expression that goes: You are what you pretend to be. This is a perfect definition of ATTITUDE. You decide your back pain is not for discussion. You may still have pain but it will be lessened by your positive attitude to manage it. Science has proven that the mind controls the

body. Choose to control it for pleasure and joy. Watch how you can mitigate your complaints.

A positive attitude motivates. A positive attitude is energetic and strong. People who are positive are happier, friendlier and much more satisfied with life. It has been proven that positivity promotes health. Complaining is not on the menu. Good attitudes need protection and admiration because it is often difficult to be positive. Some people and situations may lead you to judgments and negativity. Don't allow it. The best treatment of a negative moment is a smile, a compliment or even a hug. You disarm the negativity and you maintain your positivity.

Don't allow the negativity of others to influence you. By maintaining interest in others, you stimulate positivity. We all love to be listened to. By reaching out, reassuring and supporting you model positive attitudes. By refusing to fall into any trap of negativity, you show others how to enjoy life more fully.

It's not the reality around you; it's your attitude about it that nurtures you despite the situation. You've heard the expression: One man's junk is another's treasure. With the most nourishing ATTITUDE you can make everything, at least most of everything, into a TREASURE. Being aware of the attitude of others protects you from negative intentions. The person who is

giving you something or asking for something is doing something similar. Their attitude about the gift or the request offers the information you need to make a decision. Do you take or give? That depends on attitude. The character of a person is reflected in attitude. Connect with those whose attitude is positive, attentive and kind.

"Love is the energy of life."

EXPLANATIONS AND EXCUSES

All of our lives, ***NO*** has been considered a negative word. We've been told not to do something. We've been told no one else would ever do such a thing. ***NO*** has been an albatross around our neck. Alternatively, ***YES*** is considered a kind word. When you say ***YES*** you are accepting. Yes brings hugs and smiles and thank yous. We enjoy accolades when we say ***YES***. We fear the ramifications of refusing a request by saying ***NO.***

When you read the stories, you will understand how imperative it is that you become familiar with the necessity of ***NO***. You will learn ***NO*** is a very effective tool which proves to be protective and decisive. It signals a strong decision to avoid catastrophic results. It is often difficult, but usually very necessary. It is a clear, unambiguous statement of your needs and preferences. When faced with issues similar to these, you'll understand how careful and self-protective you need to be. You'll be thankful you chose the path to success. This information is further protection for you as you now have explicit examples of possible disasters. You now have the information to respond successfully to any challenge. You now have the information to avoid the manipulative, surreptitious requests which may be paths to destruction.

Did you lend anyone money? You didn't have to lend it. Did anyone disappoint you? Is it someone you already knew was not very reliable or efficient? Is there someone you feel anger towards, someone who has become an enemy? Do you feel the toxicity flowing from your own acquiescence? Saying ***YES*** can result in more entanglement and disappointment than saying ***NO.*** It is statistically true that ***YES*** is chosen more often and ends in pain more often. ***YES*** takes less thought and research. Be aware if the issue involves your action. Be careful. Follow the paths outlined in this book. Life will be without the anguish caused by choosing the EASY ***YES***. The trouble following a foolish, inappropriate ***yes*** is agonizing. This book enhances your sensitivity to danger and strengthens your powers to avoid it.

"It is possible to determine to live every day, one without excuses, explanations or regrets."

– Anonymous

There are simple situations which are easy to avoid. I lent a good friend my car for a few hours. Rushing to

work the next morning, I failed to notice the gas tank was empty. I was stuck in the midtown tunnel for three hours during rush hour in July. I never lent him my car again. I did not mention the ordeal I went through. Instead, I took full responsibility because I could've said ***NO.*** Jane said yes to a friend of a friend. She said, "I didn't need to check his credentials, he was recommended by a friend." He left a mess that cost Jane a fortune and a lot of time. Jane is angry with her friend. More seriously, Jane lost the friend because she angrily lashed out and blamed her. Jane could've taken responsibility by checking his credentials. She gave up the control of her own situation. It was not the friend who said ***YES***. It was Jane and she could've said ***NO.***
Nothing is the fault or responsibility of one person. You both made the deal. Remember that the next time you're on the ***YES*** side.

"It is better to offer no excuse than a bad one."
– Anonymous

In fact, the only thing standing between you and making a positive decision is the bullshit story you keep telling yourself as to why you won't say ***NO***.

My mother told her sister-in-law she could sleep at our apartment for a few days. She stayed two weeks and stole whatever she could carry. Under the guise of being kind, we put ourselves in shaky situations. Of course, there are situations that are very positive. Avoid any problems by being very careful as you make a decision. Do you vet every situation before you say ***YES***? Or, is it difficult, even impossible, for you to say ***NO?***

"YOU COULD'VE SAID NO" is a necessary book. Too many adults are in challenging, even unbearable, circumstances because they did ***not*** say ***NO***. You will be a fly on the wall of many of these victims as they say ***YES***. You will read about men and women who were not self-protective. They find themselves in situations which are horrendous and too often totally destructive. ***YES*** propels us into sad, anxious, impossible and even savage situations. ***"YOU COULD'VE SAID NO" c***learly depicts the before and after. You will read scenarios which would and could have been avoided by saying ***NO.***

PANDEMIC DIARY
Day 47
April 28, 2020

FRIENDSHIPS

The concept of being loving to those who LOVE YOU is a measure of friendship and an essential decision-making factor. There is an excellent criterion as you decide on your response. Does the person asking you to do or give something love you or do you love them? The answer YES or NO will give you essential information about motives. Your decision will need to be especially protective since it is influenced by emotional components. Years ago, I wrote a message to a dear friend. I was appalled by her foolish generosity to her family members who were not kind or even attentive to her. I wrote: "Be kind to those you love and be KINDER to those who LOVE YOU."

I've watched so many of my friends, my clients and

my own family make fools of themselves with inappropriate and unappreciated actions. Now that we have time to reflect on our lives, it might be helpful to write a letter to yourself. Concentrate on how kind you are, who you are kind to and how you've felt during and after these kind gestures.

"It is simple, my religion is kindness."
– Dali Lama

It has been amazing to discover that many of us are basically sorry for much of our kind gestures. This is not at all about expecting kudos or genuflections from those you are kind to. I hope we give with love, not with expectations. However, my question is: Why do I give and who do I give to? This book, "YOU COULD'VE SAID NO," is a direct response to those who have said yes to a potentially dangerous situation. We seem to be restricted and powerless when a friend or loved one asks for too much. When emotion is a strong component of any decision, we need to ask what is best for me at this moment. We need to learn to say NO.

Always give to those you love if the gift doesn't minimize you. Be sure that you feel good about doing it, and you will have the great satisfaction of enjoying their pleasure. Giving to those who LOVE YOU doubles your satisfaction because you feel appreciated. We need to be good to ourselves with every gesture. Giving to the person

who loves you is almost always delightful and reciprocal. Giving to those we love is a bit trickier. There are the times your antenna should go up if the person is asking too much. Be clear about the results of your agreement. What will you lose if you agree? What will you gain? Is it essential or beneficial for you? Will there be any harm if you agree? Some requests may not be beneficial for you. Be careful.

Concentrate on those fabulous friends, relatives and even neighbors who have extended themselves. Don't allow simple gestures of love to go by the wayside. Verbalize your appreciation and awareness of these gestures. In Costco, a woman was buying a bouquet of flowers. She asked if she could go ahead of the line because she had only one item. Three of us on the line agreed. She took three flowers from her bouquet and gave each person one of the flowers. It was a perfect loving gesture. She felt as good about giving as we felt. It was a lesson about generosity and kindness.

So many people have been so kind these days. We all have needs and desires that are difficult, if not impossible, to fulfill. It is so essential that we notice how often someone tries to be loving and generous. Love and attention is most delicious and appreciated.

Too often we are confronted with greed and opportunistic requests. These are the requests we are troubled by and must recognize as destructive. These are

the requests we must say NO to. I write this today as a promise to give myself more time to make decisions that benefit me. I hope to pay attention, and to respond appropriately. Awareness is a treasure. You will then notice acts of love and you will then act with generosity and appreciation.

"Love is the energy of life."

INFORMATION IS POWER

How do you make decisions? Are there questions you always ask? Is there information you insist on having? Who is asking? Do your emotions get in the way of good decisions when family or friends are asking for something? Do you take control of these decisions regardless of emotion? What are the belief systems you have which may influence your decision? Will your agreement take anything from you? Will it benefit you?

Look at your history as a decision maker. Have you been self-reliant, self-protective and wise? Have you been spontaneous? Are you too willing to say yes? Are you unaware of the ramifications of your decisions? There is one question I ask myself every time I need to decide something. I ask. ***"What is good for me at this moment?"*** Do you ask yourself this all important question? The answer to this question is imperative if you want to make a positive and protective decision. The answer will definitely help your decision? Make this question a standard part of any conversation which involves an important decision.

Knowing your strengths and weaknesses is essential information. Do you even consider yourself when a loved one is involved? Do you challenge a request even if it is from a loved one? You must recognize that some requests reek of manipulations and dire prospects. Be aware that the emotional moments are NOT the time to make any decisions. Love should never be a criterion for decision making. In fact, if love is part of the equation, you need to be especially careful. Love does not necessarily involve your own self-preservation. Although love is there, it doesn't guarantee that there is concern for you. Personal needs often ignore and even erase the feelings of love. ***"YOU COULD'VE SAID NO"*** offers an awareness of the true motivation. Too often, the need to get what is wanted, overrides any positive feelings. And too often, the need to satisfy and be loved forces us to make disastrous decisions.

During 60+ years of working with men and women, I am amazed by how much our childhood influences our everyday, moment-to-moment decisions. Learn how to recognize the pressures of your childhood. Be aware of how your childhood molded your self-image. Are you hard wired to be nice? Do you believe that the word ***YES*** is imperative because it is a nice word? Do you feel unable or fearful or undeserving to say ***NO***?

Learn that you don't need permission to say ***NO***. You do need self-confidence to make the most fruitful, beneficial and positive decisions. YOU have choices. We all have choices. Too many of us are doomed to the pain of making decisions without knowing all the facts. We feel we are not entitled to demand information. We are too anxious to please and too anxious to be loved. Pretend you are an attorney and ask the appropriate questions. Protect yourself. Shed the voices of parents or teachers who warned you to be nice. Do what is BEST for you now. No one is watching except you. Be proud. Be strong. Ask the main question: ***What is best for me at this moment?*** Don't allow the negatives of the past to be part of your future. Make choices right here in the NOW. Reject anything that is not beneficial to you.

If you change your thought process to words which take full responsibility for your actions, you'll begin to see a very positive move towards more control and self-confidence. Instead of saying, *can't*, say I *won't*. This difference in language is actually a tool to gaining confidence and decisiveness.

What in your childhood is still motivating you? Were you praised for your behavior regardless of your actions? If so, you were not given a reality check on your true abilities? If you received participation awards which are undeserved, you will be wired to believe everything you do is right and perfect. This type of belief requires you to agree to everything and anything. You need to prove you ***CAN***. Your brain is wired to accept every challenge. Your image is to always succeed and accomplish. Interestingly, this image is so deeply ingrained, you do not even perceive failures. It is called selective inattention, and is a very common defense mechanism. Saying ***yes*** is spontaneous to you, not an actual decision. It is a given that you will agree. Whatever the results, you will perceive it as good. You're trained to be a mini- robot following the demands of the moment without reason or thought.

Were you given space? Were you encouraged to *tie your own shoelaces* and *wash your own face?* If so, you have a sense of independence and trust in yourself. You are among the lucky ones with parents who nurtured self-reliance.

- You are more discriminating and curious.
- You study facts before making any decisions.
- You do consider the person making the request.
- Make sure you know the details of the situation
- Ascertain what you can lose and what you can gain.
- You are self-assured and feel the confidence it takes to probe and investigate.
- You will not make a decision in the dark.
- You need a total picture. When you struggled to *tie your own shoelaces,* you watched how to do it and learned the system. You systematically tried one way, then another. The lesson afforded you by your mother was a salient one.

If you're lucky enough to have this independent training, you are much safer than someone trained to be needy and dependent. The childhood influences are prevalent in every challenge. You will take time before any decision. You will stand firm. You will be comfortable with your decision. Confidence is built on an independent childhood.

Remember, the child is the father of the man.

How you behave is largely based upon your upbringing. We develop hard-wired belief systems, which are almost indestructible. What are yours? Be aware of how YOUR childhood is affecting you NOW. Insightful decisions are usually more positive and self-protective. These stories of victims will be warnings about your own choices. This book will be your guide. You will recognize aspects of yourself and learn when you MUST say ***NO.***

There are many clues to childhood influences. Perhaps you will recognize your own. My father told me often and lovingly that I was different. He ingrained a self confidence in me that has been a blessing and a curse. I was too sure of myself and found trouble too often. I succeeded, but at the expense of many troubling results. It is thankfully true that therapy is an answer. There is less drama in my life and a clearer knowledge of valid self-confidence. The question: "***What is best for me at this moment?***" enables me to make choices that are positive for myself.

A patient told me one of his most memorable moments. He was climbing a very steep hill in a national park. It looked very challenging and exciting. It was just the kind of activity he loved. He was 11-years-old, and like most 11-year-olds he was not afraid of anything. His father was directly behind him. "Let's wait a minute and survey our situation. What do you think," his father asked. He told me noticed the path was narrowing. The incline seemed steeper and steeper. He decided that he and his father should retreat. They'd had enough adventure for the moment. His father instilled the benefit of being cautious. He didn't order him or even tell him. He wisely demonstrated the art of making positive decisions. He showed him how to use information wisely while making decisions. He is hard wired to carefully and scrupulously gather the facts, examine them from every angle and then decide. He is emotionally and financially successful. His childhood training continues to guide him.

THE TRAGIC DECISION

Madge's childhood was painful, even cruel. She was physically abused, neglected and betrayed. Many promises were broken, and many disappointments were inflicted upon her. She was promised that if she came out from under the bed, she would not be hit again. She was beaten with a strap as soon as she emerged. Her ability to trust was destroyed. Imagine how deeply she was scarred. Today she will make choices to avoid pain. Her psychological strengths need to avoid any connection to the negative factors in her childhood. She does not trust anyone, especially NOT herself. When asked her opinion she freezes like a deer caught in the headlights. Her decisions are without thought except to avoid any immediate discomfort. Her answer is usually, "It's up to you —what you think best." This type of response is a reflection of her need to stay out of it. She is frightened of being blamed and punished. She is frightened of being accountable. She rationalizes that what is eventually DONE TO HER will be a far better choice than she would make herself. Knowing this about her childhood, you can understand how she could have made such a destructive decision.

She didn't have the confidence or courage to say ***NO*** *to* her son Harold. Under the guise of love, he literally destroyed his mother. He demanded she agree to his evil proposal. Her fear of making a mistake and the pressure he posed were her downfalls. Madge gave him permission to destroy her when she said ***YES***. She was unable to fight. You will read her very tragic story.

I have worked with thousands of men and women seeking solutions to the vagaries of life. So many create rather than avoid their suffering. So many are totally responsible for the pain they feel. We all seek answers to difficulties. This book gives the answers. More importantly, this book explains how serious your own decisions are. Reading this book offers you warning signals and information that will keep you from making bad decisions. If you don't allow your emotions to cloud your decisions and you follow the techniques and skills offered in this book, you will prevent any possibility of a negative decision.

Madge's son Harold is a shameless, inconsiderate and vicious man. His plan for his mother is an example of inhumanity.

THE TRUTH SHOWS ITS UGLY HEAD, IF ONLY WE OPEN OUR EYES

Harold said he felt he was being very generous. He offered Madge a life of luxury, a full-time housekeeper and a boat she could not operate. He ignored all that she would lose if she said ***YES*** to him. Did he even contemplate what she would be losing? Did he really believe he was offering benefits? When she hesitated, feebly stating her own wishes, he became surly and even offensive. He told her it would ***not*** be in his best interests financially if she refused. He would lose an IRS deduction. He insisted it would hurt him if she refused his generous offer.

Was Harold's suggestion really BEST for Madge? Did he show any respect for her needs? Was she better off away from a wonderfully active, fun lifestyle? Did he realize her friends would be 40 miles away, and barely, if ever, see her? Did he understand the treasures she would be losing? Did he care?

Madge was alone, miserable and furious with herself and with her son. Walking the distance to the kitchen was exhausting. Madge kept food in a small refrigerator. She used a microwave, and usually ate alone in bed. Her son visited only twice when she was alive. When he was in Florida, he had dinner dates. He went to see shows and took boating trips with friends. Madge was not invited. He was worried that it was too much for her.

Devious as it was, he quickly had her home sold, her belongings auctioned and was, "holding the funds for her." He claimed that the IRS gave him a financial benefit because his mother was to live in the house. The IRS gives no such benefit.

Can a son be so evil? Can a tax deduction be so essential? Madge's story is one of manipulation and cruelty. We MUST be wary and put ourselves FIRST. If she had said ***NO*** she'd be playing bridge right now. Madge was not given a second chance. She died 11 months after saying, ***"YES,"*** to Harold. The doctor should have written "Cause of Death – Broken Heart." Madge was 83 years young.

Are you shocked? Do you find this impossible to believe? Try an experiment for yourself and research the incidence of parental abuse. Ask your friends if they have been abused. This book will help YOU and others from doing damage to yourself. Make decisions on ALL the facts. Remember you have the right to say ***NO.***

Invariably there are many childhood experiences which continue to influence us. A mother who is nervous and in need of constant attention will invoke feelings of inadequacy and need in her child. Such a woman has very little left to give her son. The child is emotionally starved and abused. He will seek love and attention in every way possible. Bad decisions will plague him. A childhood deprived of a loving touch is cruel and defeating. It is difficult to rise above the need for love. It is sad that so many of us have suffered such childhoods. Many of us are burdened with the pain of inadequate parenting. We travel along the road desperately searching for some acceptance. Achieving such validation is usually short lived because the price is very costly.

A childhood without love has a powerfully negative effect on the adult. Was there physical abuse, neglect and betrayal? Were promises broken and many disappointments suffered? This child will make choices to avoid pain, not recognizing how much worse a bad decision can be. There is no trust for anyone and especially not for himself. The decision will be what he thinks is easiest, quickest and without any responsibility. His answer is usually, "It's up to you. What do you think is best?" This type of response is a reflection of his need to stay out of it. He is frightened of being blamed and punished. He is frightened of being accountable. If something is done to him, he is safe because he is not responsible. Being responsible is worse for him than anything done to him. He is pitiful and disrespected. He feels ashamed. He has no pride. His fears control him. His childhood is his nemesis. Is there someone in your life who suffers in this way?

As you read, you will recognize aspects of your own motivations. Go down memory lane. What was your childhood like? Did you feel love, rejection, support, admiration or neglect? Whatever you felt is the foundation of your feelings and behavior now. Discover what was done in your childhood that influences you now. It never goes away until you identify it, grab it and take control. Awareness is 95% of the battle. If you have self-doubt, take time before you make decisions. If you have fearful memories, take MORE time. These insights will intensify your own strengths, and instill in your psyche your right to say ***NO***.

It is imperative that you understand your own process of making decisions. There are many standard questions that you can use in this regard. What is the process of your decision making? Is it fear of being disliked? Is it fear of losing a relationship? Is it a self-image that denies you your personal power?

A perfect example of the control our childhood yields over us is the story of Liz and her son Roger. Liz was never emotionally validated. She doesn't remember a word of praise or acceptance. She constantly played the good girl in an effort to be recognized. Her son found her

Achilles heel and played on her good girl image. She felt that she had to give him everything he asked for in order to maintain Roger's love. Everyone else was mortified by how she destroyed her own life. You will find Liz's story horrendous. It is a story of vicious mistreatment. It is a story of the unrelenting demands that she satisfy her son while denying herself. Her self-confidence was so damaged that she was weakened to the point of being incapacitated. She was unable to see the reality. She was too denigrated to change the nightmare. At each juncture, she chose destruction. She ***COULD'VE SAID NO.***

A ROLE MODEL FOR THE BAD SEED

"Destroy the seed of evil or it will grow to be your ruin." – Aesop

This is a story of Roger's greed and his mother Liz's blindness to his evil character. Roger was always first in her heart and decisions. He stole from her. He lied incessantly. He never had a job and he took what he could as often as he could. This was a saga that lasted 40 years and that ended more tragically than imaginable. Liz's childhood of neglect was the impetus for her self-destructive behavior.

Liz inherited money from her longtime companion. Unfortunately, Liz and Roger had a joint bank account. She gave him her power of attorney. She gave him full rein to steal whatever he wanted, without any protection or limitations. He had Liz move in with him, telling her that he did not want her to be alone. He sold her house and put the money into his own account. After three months, he told Liz she should live with her daughter Gracie during the cold winter months. It was an excuse to be rid of her.

Liz went to live with Gracie thinking that it would be temporary. Gracie was the neglected child in the family. She was always passed over for Roger's needs and developed intense anger against both Roger and her mother. Liz had been living with Gracie for the past five years. Roger did not want her to return to his home. He said his wife didn't want her living with them.

Gracie tried to change Liz's bank account and address since Liz was living with her. The joint checking account was empty. He had taken more than $250,000 from the account. Roger had been cashing Liz's social security checks for months. It was impossible for Gracie to take any legal action against Roger or to recover any of the property he'd stolen. Liz had given Roger her power of attorney. Since Liz gave the power of attorney willingly and refused to withdraw it, the power is ironclad. Liz gave Roger total legal control, including the right to steal her money and sell her property.

Elder abuse agencies were contacted. Social Services and three different attorneys were contacted. Nothing could be done. Gracie was Liz's only hope. Her social security check was not adequate to cover any decent adult housing. Gracie, the child who was totally neglected in favor of Roger, was now caring for her mother. Liz's health has deteriorated rapidly. At first she was forgetful and depressed. She is now suffering severe dementia, refuses to communicate at all and has retreated to sleeping 90% of the time. Gracie fed and showered her. She took her for medical care and even had her nails and hair done professionally. Liz showed no appreciation or recognition. Roger called once or twice a year. At first, Liz spoke to him lovingly and happily, although she didn't favor anyone else with such kindness. Now, she is unable to respond, even to him.

It is said that history repeats itself if you don't learn from it. For a few years, Liz continued to defend Roger. She spoke of loving him, and incredibly she spoke of trusting him. Even after he rejected her visits to his home, after he didn't call and after she knew he had taken 100% of her financial life, she continued to praise him.

If not for Gracie, Liz would be living in a senior facility which accepts social security. I'm sure you realize the conditions in that environment. Liz's social security is $850.00 a month. Think of Liz before signing anything or saying yes to any request. Be especially wary if the term power of attorney rears its ugly head. Once you sign it, it is difficult to go back. If you do sign it, be sure to delineate the area covered. Also be sure it is reversible. Better yet, don't give the power to anyone. Liz found out the hard way, but she continued her faith in Roger. This faith has rendered her helpless and pitiful. Her dementia is all-inclusive, affecting behavior and thoughts. She was isolated within herself, unable to face what she'd done to herself and how she'd been betrayed.

Of course this is extreme. It is also a totally true story. Yes, she did it to herself. Yes, her family, sisters, daughter and friends begged her for years to recognize the evil of this man. Yes, she rejected anyone who spoke against him. Yes, she was totally responsible. Yes, there are many like her. She is paying the heaviest price. She has dementia. Roger has abandoned her. Gracie was her angel now. Liz's realization that Gracie was never treated well was probably contributing to her illness. I'm sure that somewhere in her confused and damaged brain Liz appreciates her daughter. She doesn't have the ability to show it. Reading this book is a lesson for everyone. Don't be burdened with illness born of bad decisions. Don't accept the resulting pain infused with every bad decision.

It is sad but true that Bloodlines do not always flow with love, respect and consideration. Too often these lines are clogged with evil and greed. It is up to each of us to protect ourselves from bad decisions, regardless of the possible source. Be as good to yourself as possible and at all times.

You will be faced with infinitely varied requests. Your son needs money. Your sister wants to live with you. Your daughter wants you to live with her. Your needy friend is asking ***again***. Suddenly, you're in a terrible situation. We are all confronted with requests. Sometimes we are confronted with demands. We are given advice and suggestions on how and what and when if a problem arises. How we react to these pressures is the determining factor. Will you protect yourself and maintain your own integrity? Will you fade away into a script written by another? Your choice is determined by YOU and only YOU. It is YOU who will reap the benefits or the horrors of your decisions. Remember to ask ***what is best for me at this moment?***

Ask yourself how you feel about a request. Are you afraid of being disliked? Is anger something to avoid at all costs? If you make a mistake, are you guilty? There is a fear of being judged and a fear of losing a relationship. There are so many fears and personal issues which hinder or encourage decisions. Too often we are not aware of our own motivations. When faced with a decision that will result in changes in your lifestyle, be cautious. Don't think that it doesn't matter. Don't rationalize that you don't care. Pay attention. Learn all the facts and protect yourself. "I don't care" or "it doesn't matter" or the infamous "whatever" are words which are usually self-destructive. These words are crutches to lean on while avoiding your power to be confident and taking control.

Ask your questions. Take time and be your own best friend.

- Is it so difficult to decide what is best for YOU when a request is made?

- Why do we continue to create excuses to allow others to abuse us?

- Are we blind to the truth that many requests are abusive? Do we deny that someone we love and trust is capable of wanting more than we ***should give***?

- Do they ever ask for what they know is ***not*** best for us? Can they be that selfish? Yes they are. You will see many sad situations which could and should have been avoided. Most essentially and most difficult is accepting that love is not always a factor. There are possibilities that your response can have devastating results for YOU.

The truly sad truth is that destructive behavior is repeated again and again. We do ***not*** take the time to examine our ***YES***. We want to say ***NO.*** We know ***YES*** will not end well. But we fall prey to our emotional pressures.

When presented with the difficulty of a decision, our body takes control. We experience heaving, breathing with a tight chest and a clogged throat. Imagine a child, a parent or a beloved friend is asking something of you. You are very aware that this request is wrong, even hurtful. The thought that you are being asked is painful. But, the ***NO*** remains buried in a distant area of your mature brain. Every fiber of your being is saying, Sorry**,** ***NONONONO***. Yet too often anxieties drive us into truly horrible situations. The need to be agreeable and to be loved is imbedded deeply in our psyche.

It is especially difficult to believe that a loved one is asking something of you that is ***NOT BEST*** for you.

- After all, how can we believe that a daughter's request that you live with her is not what she thinks is best for you?

- Can a loving son expect you to leave your home and friends because it's ***better*** for you?

Before you decide any change, you MUST consider all aspects of what you are being asked! Dr. Hans Selye is a well-respected and avid researcher of the human condition. Dr. Selye has developed a hierarchy of stressful situations. He concludes that moving is the most stressful of all stressors. I suggest that you be especially careful if any request involves changing your environment.

You are reading the results of these catastrophic decisions. You will be amazed as you learn about how often healthy adults make drastic mistakes and actually choose to be abused. The best learning tool is experience. Seeing these experiences, you will realize there are always alternative choices. Taking time before making any decision has been proven to be an excellent path to better decisions. You will see the joy and relief of those who did learn when and how to say ***NO***. Unfortunately, you will also see the misery and burdens of those who could not or would not make decisions in their own favor.

These situations are all real, shared by clients, friends and colleagues during the past 60+ years. The decisions, requests and results are true. The emotions and tragedies resulting from the decisions are real. The underlying causes of these bad decisions are surprisingly similar. In the strong, confident decision makers, the psychological strengths are obvious. In the weaker and less confident, there are also psychological similarities. The major difference is how these messages are dealt with. These are examples of obliteration, destruction and endless self-flagellation.

Do you imagine you would or could ever make such horrific decisions? Is there anything in these personal accounts triggering something in you? These situations are not rare. They are part of the human experiences faced throughout our lives. Thoughts of your own strength and confidence as protections from these types of problems may be flawed. Strength and confidence can be whittled down under the guise of love. Be sure of who you are. Do you know if you are confident and self-protective?

You may recognize yourself in many of these true stories. You will learn skills to enforce self-love, pride and determination. You will learn that saying ***NO*** is a giant step towards more comfort, happiness and a less stressful life. These pages are a roadmap of effective, simple techniques which offer safety. You will gain awareness, powerful paths to confidence and the infinite truth that you CAN AND MUST make positive choices. You are now learning the horrors suffered because ***NO*** was not the answer. ***"YOU COULD'VE SAID NO"*** is the tool fueling your power box. It is your power to avoid negative possibilities. This is your master plan to utilize confidence, determination and positivity in all of your decisions.

THE POWER OF YES AND NO

"Resentment is like drinking poison and hoping it will kill your enemy." – Nelson Mandela

This quote is most important in the decision making process. Is it ***YES*** or is it ***NO?*** AND most importantly — ***WHAT IS BEST FOR YOU?***

Robert and his grown daughter Kimberly came to see me for therapy. Robert was a man of distinction. He held the title as a person with total well thought out control of his own needs and his own decisions. He used ***YES*** and ***NO*** as adroitly as the flip of a TV station. His choices were completely dependent on the information he carefully gathered on each situation.

Robert thought things through and made his decisions based on facts. He was a perfect example of a person truly in charge of himself, his needs and his responsibilities. His answer to this question was the ultimate deciding factor: *"What is BEST for me at this moment?"*

At that point he knew he needed therapy because of what had occurred with his daughter.

He recounted several very graphic examples of his self-loving relationship with his daughter. He bought a house for Kimberly to live in while she attended Brown University. It was a shrewd investment since he would probably make a profit when he sold the house. When Kimberly decided she wanted to invite friends to live with her, he refused and said, *"NO."* He considered the possible damage of several young people living rent free. However, he also said ***"YES"*** if she preferred to live in the dorm.

Kimberly accused him of unkindness and totally uncaring. He asked her to be clear in her thinking. After all, he gave her choices. Satisfy her need for company in the dorm or stay in the house without sharing it. She decided to stay in the house. When Robert discovered that three others were living with her, he sent her the payment book on the mortgage for the house. He had protected himself by putting the mortgage in her name. He knew he was not taking a risk. If she didn't pay the mortgage, the deed would defer to him since he owned the deed. Another example of how well he planned and how carefully he protected himself.

The scenario was fascinating. He was a good father. He took responsibility for his daughter by paying for her college expenses and providing for safe housing. He did so within his strict boundaries, to always protect himself. Although She finally decided to stay in the dorm, he said ***"NO"*** to her request to pay the cost of the dorm until she paid the outstanding mortgage. Robert knew that Kimberly had a trust fund that was at her disposal. He also knew that she hated to spend her own money on anything. She was a piece of work. Kimberly shouted at him to stop teaching her these stupid lessons. He was thrilled that she knew it was a lesson hard learned.

Kimberly continued to feel inclined to entitlement and privilege. At times, she became angry even spiteful. To his credit Robert did not become angry or change his decision making style. When she became engaged, he pulled out all the stops and funded the spectacular wedding she'd always wanted. They were close for years and were seen as the idyllic father and daughter. Robert relished their relationship and was thrilled. The day came he was going to become a grandfather. He had no idea of what was coming.

On that day Kimberly informed Robert that he should **NOT** come to the hospital. She and her husband wanted to bond with the baby privately. Robert understood and expected it would be a short wait. She finally called him and said she had a little boy and instructed him to postpone seeing the newborn until they left the hospital.

Robert was disappointed, however, impatient and went to the hospital hoping that Kimberly would realize his need to see his grandson.

He was told to leave and wait for an invitation.

Kimberly's in-laws were with her, holding the baby when Robert's son-in-law blocked the doorway to the room. The shock and pain, the incredible act of cruelty astounded Robert. He left the hospital and suffered for months trying to understand what happened.

You may think there must be a reason for Kimberly's behavior. I found one. Kimberly is probably the most narcissistic person I have ever worked with. The world has to revolve around her and she created rules and regulations to fit her needs. Narcissists do not experience empathy. She seemed to have no idea that she was hurting her father as seriously as slicing his throat.

Robert enjoyed the next year with his son and his grandchildren. They speculated about Kimberly and came to understand her psychological limitations. During therapy, both father and daughter were able to spit out the poisonous anger and quell most of the sadness. More importantly they learned to accept Kimberly's narcissist tendencies and live a healthy and contented life despite their loss.

I mentioned that Robert was a poster boy for making self-loving decisions. Therapy was one of those decisions. Amazingly enough, when Kimberly called to invite him to dinner, he chose to accept. He decided to enjoy whatever Kimberly was able to share, and not deny himself their relationship. Perhaps it's a miracle or a great example of acceptance and the purity of love. They were a family again and they never mentioned the hospital incident.

They spoke only of the present and the pleasure of the moment.

A famed author and brilliant guru, Krishnamurti, said, "There are many things that are better left unsaid." Robert said ***"NO"*** when he needed to for his own needs. He also said ***"YES"*** despite the past, because of his own needs NOW. He is an example of courage and pride as well as intelligence and true love.

Saying ***YES*** is NOT a sign of weakness if there were problems. It is actually a sign of strength if you say ***YES*** because it is BEST for YOU. It is a basic truth that you cannot change the past. It is also a basic truth that it is most beneficial to forget the negatives of the past. In order to improve the present, and the future, it is best to look ahead to what is NOW.

"Remove the suffering and you get the happiness." – The Buddha

There are many brilliant quotes which teach the efficacy and necessity of forgiveness. One especially excellent reason to forgive, is to receive the pleasures available. Robert understood this as he decided on behaviors that were best for him and his family. This is very admirable. There is a place of importance for ***NO*** if problems are prevented. There is also a place for ***YES*** if benefits follow.

PANDEMIC DIARY
Day 78
May 29, 2020

FORGIVENESS

"Forgiveness is the fragrance that the violet sheds on the heel that has crushed it."
– Mark Twain

Today I think it is necessary to write about an essential path to health. Being quarantined, feeling controlled and being isolated are unhealthy restrictions. We are in this until the virus is obliterated. We need to use this time to maintain our health. Since our situation is not as wonderful as we'd like, let us make the results even more wonderful than we hope. Several of the emails I receive are questions and statements about anger and resentment. Some people are anxious, sensitive and unhappy. They overreact and become negative because someone said the wrong word or acted

unpleasantly.

We need to let go. We need to hold on to all or any positives that come our way. If we perceive something as negative, trust the perception. LET IT GO.

"Forgiveness is not an occasional act, but a constant attitude." – Mahatma Gandhi

One of these barriers is the inability to forgive. Too often we rationalize that forgiveness is weak. It is giving in. The anger within is justified. Too often we think that forgiveness is NOT possible. If you make these excuses and refuse forgiveness, you create barriers of communication and connections. If YOU refuse to forgive, you give power and control to the offender. IF you give away your ability to control, you give away a powerful piece of yourself. It is a fact that withholding forgiveness is opening a door to toxicity.

The negativity is poisonous to your immune system. The truth is that forgiveness does not include retaining a relationship with the oppressor. To forgive is FOR GIVING a release from blame —a release from responsibility to the offender. Mainly, it is a release from YOUR pain. It is actually a cleansing of your own rage. It is also recognition that you have the power to choose positive and healthy behaviors. It is actually releasing your own distress. It is not positive or productive to

attribute blame. It is NOT within your power to attribute evil. IT IS within your power to protect yourself by NOT holding on to the offense, AND by LETTING GO.

"Love is the energy of life."

MY HUSBAND OR MY DAUGHTER

"Knowing when to walk away is wisdom. Being able to is courage. Walking away with your head held high is dignity." – Anonymous

Cindi wrote her mother a devastating letter about her father. She said: "Mom, dad has behaved unacceptably with my little girls. I cannot allow him to ever see them again. If you want to visit us, you're welcome, but without him. Love, Cindi."

The letter from Cindi to her mother, Shelly, shocked me. Shelley described her terrible predicament and I imagined the horror of how dreadful she felt. It was even worse when she told me that Cindi refused to explain anything further. Shelley was extremely depressed.

How could she decide to visit Cindi and the girls when her husband, Ken, was not welcome? Why would Cindi accuse her own father of behaving unacceptably?

What could he possibly have done? The entire family loved Ken and remarked about what a great grandfather he was.

Fourteen members of the family were at a lake resort for a fabulous fun filled week. Everyone noticed Ken's energy with the girls and the fun they were having. When they were together there was lots of swimming, boating, ice cream parties, laughing and hugging. It was impossible that Ken was banned from his granddaughters.

Cindi refused to offer any reasons, but this remark gave Shelley a lot of information: *"Take it or leave it, my husband comes first for me."* Shelley then knew her son-in-law was responsible for Cindi's decision.

Shelley and Ken were very wealthy. They have always been very generous to both of their children and their five grandchildren. Each received an annual stipend from their successful business. Shelley wanted to cut Cindi from their will and end the bonus each child received annually. Ken refused. He felt that whatever Cindi was doing, he wanted to continue to support and love her and the girls. A testimony to Ken's loving character.

The final decision was up to Shelley. She continued to see Cindi and her grandchildren.

She took them to dinners and luncheons.

She took them to ballet and karate class.

She took them on extravagant shopping excursions.

She bought tickets to shows the girls would enjoy. Shelley spent as much time with the girls as Cindi would allow.

Her decision was to say ***"YES"*** to all of Cindi's demands. Her decision was to continue to enjoy her granddaughters. Her decision was to leave Ken aching for the joy of his girls each time Shelley went to visit them.

Shelley was very conflicted, but ignoring Ken's feelings, she catered to her own. One night Shelley noticed the girls always ordered expensive steak or lobster for dinner. They also always ordered dessert and extra ice cream. On top of that, they ordered a fruit plate to take home. The bill was always handed to Shelley because she was their personal bank.

There was no reciprocity. Cindi's husband never offered anything, not even a "Thank you." She also noticed that Cindi was always with the girls. It became obvious that the girls were not allowed to be alone with their grandmother. Reality began to pull at her. Cindi was policing their relationship. Nothing was said or done with the girls without their mother or father's presence and approval.

Shelley felt like a fool. She wasn't even enjoying the company of her grandchildren. The atmosphere was stifling. Conversation was sporadic as they were not at all spontaneous or cheerful. The girls behaved as though they were fearful of their parents disapproval. Shelley noticed a discomfort at being hugged and glances at their mother to see if hugging was allowed. Questions were avoided and replies were monosyllabic. "How was school?" "OK."

The possibility of not seeing the girls seemed to be a relief rather than pain and disappointment. The acceptance that the situation was unviable was finally developing in Shelley's mind. They were young enough to have fun and play together, but the only activity Cindi allowed was a luxury dinner or a shopping trip with no financial limits. Shelley was so distraught and confused she began to withdraw. She asked herself, "Is my withdrawal finally evidence that I'm waking up to the truth?"

She also became more aware of Ken's deep sadness. He had no idea what he had done to be denied the pleasure of two wonderful grandchildren. The girls had been a special part of his life. He felt betrayed and abused. He had no outlet. It seemed to Ken that Shelley was oblivious to his pain.

Shelley was finally aware of the reaction to this situation. She asked Ken if her visits to the girls were a problem for him. Ken began to sob. During one of our therapy sessions, I asked Shelley to summarize her life for the past eight months. She was very honest and recognized that Cindi had indeed betrayed her father. She also recognized her disappointment at continuing to support all of the luxuries she'd allowed. She said she would demand an explanation of Ken's banishment from the girls. She wondered if there was some other explanation for labeling

Ken as inappropriate. Finally, she tearfully admitted that in reality the girls had been taken from her as well.

I wish, for Shelley's sake, that she'd cut all connection with the misery caused by Cindi. I wish Cindi admitted it was ridiculous to accuse her father of being mean to the girls. I wish the yearly stipend was removed and Ken was validated at being innocent of any wrongdoing towards the girls. I wish Shelley energized her self-esteem and set limits on her unappreciated generosity. I wish the best for Shelley, but it doesn't seem possible.

It's been almost eight years since I first met Shelley. Cindi finally admitted that her husband was jealous of Ken because his daughters seemed to have more fun with their grandpa. Cindi admitted that her husband warned her he never wanted to see her father again…or he would divorce her. Cindi also said she wished she'd been divorced before blindly hurting her father so cruelly. Cindy had become submissive and totally diminished. Her own joy and personality was evaporated. Her need for keeping the appearance of a happy marriage destroyed the family spirit for a long time.

This story is quite a lesson for everyone. We all need to maintain our self-image. It is more essential that we protect our SELF-ESTEEM even more. What others think of us is of course important. What we think of ourselves is crucial. We exaggerate our confidence or diminish our fears. Accepting the reality is our strength. When Cindi was threatened with the failure of her marriage and being without her man, she caved. Needing to present the picture of financial and emotional success, she thrust her father into pain and out of her life. Unimaginable? No. Cindi's behavior is not rare at all. We give in to save what we insatiably embrace. We give in to the culprit who has convinced us that he/she is indispensable. Think about yourself and ask, "How often am I so foolish? Who is my obsession? What demands would I refuse? What demands have I accepted?"

Shelley and her husband have weathered the storm. They remain partners who are more firmly united than ever before. Everyone knows not to try to come between them. The pain of their mistakes is the thread that weaves their love tightly and visibly. Remember, Reagan and Nancy? Their love was as invincible as the Reagan's.

The girls are young adults now and have apologized for the past. They love their grandparents and choose to be with them often. Cindi does not interfere with their plans. However Cindi is a persona non grata to Shelley and Ken. Forgiveness does not mean inclusion in your life. They are not friends, nor do they profess any love or understanding for what Cindi's done. They speak to her and attend family functions together. Some behaviors cannot be undone. The pain is impressed too deeply to be completely obliterated.

"The moving finger writes, and having written moves on. Nor all thy piety nor all thy wit, can cancel half a line of it." –Kahlil Gibran

If we could go back, the story would be simple. If Cindi had said ***"NO"*** to her husband –none of this would have happened. She would probably not have been divorced if she encouraged him as a good father and discouraged his jealousy and accusations as weak. If she'd encouraged and enhanced his adequacy he may have developed self-esteem and given up the need to blame someone else. If Shelley had said ***"NO"*** to Cindy, this could have been avoided. If Shelley had insisted that Ken see the girls, they would be smiling about this now.

Remember that a behavior to satisfy a weakness or a fault is not productive or even kind. Remedy the weakness or the fault, don't enhance it or encourage it as Cindi did. ***NO*** is a very powerful word. It creates happy situations and prevents unhappiness. In fact ***YES*** is often a thief of time and contentment.

In each decision there is a crucial ***NO***. It is usually the safer way to go. Reminisce about the forks in the road you have faced. Examine the decisions you've made. Think about this:

Do you ever feel it would have been best for you if you had said ***"NO?"***

Are you more aware and more determined to make good, self-loving decision?

Do you take your time and think about each decision?

Do you follow the decision making rules?

Do you ask the right questions?

Do you obtain all the pertinent information, and envision the possible results?

I know when to stop. I know when to let go. BUT I KNOW, is quite different from I CAN. And ***I CAN*** is quite different from ***I WILL***.

Can you say no? Will you say no?

This a profound truth. Decision making is your **POWER**. Your decision is **YOUR FUTURE**.

MY SON, THE ATTORNEY

Ilene and Evan owned a successful travel agency. Their son, Josh, asked to join the firm. He hated being a lawyer and wanted to be closer to his parents. He opened a second office and became very successful. He asked for a partnership saying he had big dreams for the agency. It seemed fair. They loved their son. Finances were not an issue. They gave him a 50% partnership. After all, they did have two agencies.

The next red flag was the request for a power of attorney. Again, Ilene and Evan agreed. Josh invited his parents to dinner at a very elite restaurant. They were thrilled, intending to celebrate the successes they enjoyed. They were also very confused. Josh handed them a set of keys. He told them the party was for their retirement. He said the keys were to a penthouse on Singer Island in Florida. He told them he intended to pay their moving expenses.

Ilene and Evan are still bewildered. How did this happen? Why did they allow it to happen? Josh actually sold their home and arranged to move their furniture to Florida. Devastated and hopelessly depressed, they moved. Their penthouse was breathtaking, with a view of the ocean. It was just a few steps from the beach. It sounds good to the onlooker. Not surprisingly, Josh believes he is a wonderful son. Josh's wife is furious with Ilene and Evan because they don't appreciate what's been done for them.

This is certainly a sad sample of the expression, "there are two sides to every story." Ilene and Evan were both under 60 years old. They lost pride in success. They miss the pleasure of working with their customers and the thrill of being productive. It was ripped away by a "loving" son. Or, it was given away by trusting and foolish parents. It is incredibly hard to believe yet true.

This story is unusual, because much of what Ilene did is understandable. She and Evan were thrilled that Josh wanted to work with them. They took it as a compliment to their success. They also imagined lots of time together and a perfect bonding. It is almost impossible to anticipate such a conclusion to the gracious act of taking your son into your business. There were many other steps which were blaring red warning signals. Why give Josh a partnership? What were they trying to prove? Even more incredible is granting him a power of attorney. Kindness and family trust can be given with boundaries legal and otherwise. Protection could have been part of the involvement. They could have protected themselves and been generous as well. They could've said ***NO***, many times along the way.

Thanks to some therapy and the powerful love Ilene and Even have for each other, they retained their dignity and their ambition. They have a small but popular and profitable consulting firm. They advise people who are moving to other countries or other states. They understand the pain and anxiety involved in moving. They understand other cultures and opportunities in other places. They understand and are easily involved in caring for others. Their empathy, knowledge and incredible generosity are the wheels that carry them forward. The strength is in their love for each other and the self-confidence they developed as a couple. Ilene was able to overcome her childhood within Evan's arms. Evan agreed to all of Josh's requests because he thought Ilene wanted to. He always did everything for Ilene. He thought she wanted to say ***YES*** to Josh. Love is truly the energy of life. Evan told me jokingly that Josh is not their attorney.

If you are fooled or taken advantage of by a loved one, don't beat yourself up. Don't allow yourself to continue to be a victim. In all of these stories, the abuse is cruel and damaging. ***NO*** is the word which will avoid so much. If you're a victim, the only successful possibility is for you to forgive and go on to better decisions and better relationships. Do not remain a victim. Let go.

THE NIGHTMARE OF YES

Learning through experience is very effective. Learning through the experience of others is also very effective. A child will not touch a stove if he is burned himself or if he sees another person screech in pain as he touches the stove. As you read these heartfelt stories, you see the painful results of a ***YES***. If you comply to the wrong question, the wrong person and at the wrong time, you will feel the horror of not being protective. Let's examine a few additional real-life situations. Read how healthy adults choose abuse which could have been easily avoided with a ***NO***. As you recognize the possibility that there are alternative choices, you will have an a-ha moment and the future will seem brighter. Many have empowered themselves with the choice of ***NO***. The stories of joy and relief are motivations for being self-protective. Unfortunately, you have seen much of the misery when the victims would or would not make decisions in their own favor.

These situations are all real, shared by clients, friends and colleagues during the past 60+ years. The decisions, requests and results are real. The emotions resulting from decisions are real. The underlying causes of these decisions are surprisingly similar. In the strong, confident decision makers, the psychological strengths are obvious. In the weaker and less confident, there are also psychological similarities. The major difference is how these messages are dealt with, enforced or obliterated.

You probably recognized yourself or others in many of these true stories. Situations range from going to a movie or a restaurant you don't like, to leaving your home and a life you love because a child thought it best for you. You've learned skills to enforce self-love, pride and determination. You know that saying ***"NO"*** is often a giant step towards being comfortable, being happier and being less stressed. Saying ***"NO"*** is often necessary to maintain a loving relationship.

These pages are a roadmap of effective, simple techniques which offer safety. You gain awareness with each story. You enhance your confidence and recognize that you MUST make positive self-protective choices. You've been an investigator and voyeur. You've learned of some horrible situations because ***NO*** was not their answer.

"***YOU COULD'VE SAID NO***" is your power to avoid such possibilities. This is your master plan for confidence, determination and positivity in all of your decisions. It's your ammunition.

"Each decision reflects your infinite power."
– Carole Altman

PANDEMIC DIARY

Day 96
June 16, 2020

TRUST

"It is simple. Kindness is my religion."
– Dalai Lama

Good Morning and thank you for your support. It is incredibly encouraging to know that many of you truly enjoy the information I've shared. I will continue to offer some of these ideas, although it will not be on any definite schedule. I intend to respond to suggestions and questions. Most recently a question I received was very intriguing.

Why do some people have a hard time with relationships? The person further asked if there was a reason she kept losing relationships? She added that too often she had no idea what happened to end the relationship.

There is a psychological phenomenon I call "self-love deficit." This pattern is frequent and always destructive. If you do not like yourself, you cannot accept anyone who actually manifests an attraction to you. You begin to wonder why or how this person actually enjoys your company. You begin to mistrust any compliments or gestures of kindness.

The defense mechanism we all have and actually need for self-protection begins to kick in. Rather than accept the attention and trust it, we rationalize that there is nothing wrong with you. Therefore, if this person is being kind to you there must be some Machiavellian motive for his behavior. Your thoughts turn to his problems. There must be something wrong with him if his behavior motivates my suspicions. I certainly don't want to be involved with someone who suffers such serious problems. I must end this relationship before he hurts me even more. I must find a way to get rid of him in a way that clears me of any blame. I begin to destroy the relationship with lateness, rudeness, inattention, coldness, etc. I do anything and everything until he ends the relationship . My suspicions about his motives justify my negative behaviors and ending the relationship. The question commonly raised, is: "What happened?"

You have no awareness of the psychological dynamics causing these irrational thoughts and behaviors. There is only the deep seated fear that you don't deserve kindness. If you feel good or happy, you become discombobulated and seek a solution for this discomfort. It never occurs to you your own feeling of unworthiness is causing this.

This may sound convoluted and just psychobabble. However, it is one of the serious flaws in our self-image which is so destructive. Self-love, Self-appreciation, Self-pride, is rare, and if we feel it, we're not supposed to show it. If I love myself, I'm a braggart, I'm selfish, I'm arrogant. If I love myself I'm a narcissist and a jerk.

Positive and loving feelings are difficult for many of us to accept, especially towards ourselves. We don't nurture the feelings to avoid the possible criticisms. Instead we nurture the negatives which produce approval and acceptance. One of the most popular trends in comedy is self-deprecation. It may be funny to some, but it is most destructive. The result is that those who truly have a weakness support the weakness and it flourishes. The loss of relationships is a very common result when we lack self-love.

Make a chart of your positives. Write down everything good and wonderful about YOU. Flaunt the feelings and begin to appreciate your infinite value and share all your goodies. Realize how worthy you are of love, attention and friendships. Do NOT judge yourself as undeserving. Accept that you deserve love.

That which is given is what is what is received.

GIVE. RECEIVE. Do this with open arms and deep thankfulness. Appreciate yourself and cherish your value. Bestow the truth of The Dali Lama, and be kind. Trust is an essential aspect of all relationships.

"Love is the energy of life."

DAUGHTER TO AVOID

My friend, Enid, almost made a major mistake. Her daughter Shirley was not loving or caring. Shirley suggested Enid and Sid move to Ohio to be closer to her. Shirley knew they both loved living in Las Vegas. They did not want to move to a senior facility in Ohio. They knew that their daughter was not particularly easy to be around. They knew it would be quite a loss to leave Las Vegas. They also felt that perhaps she sincerely wanted to be closer to them at this point in their lives. They were confused and fearful. Enid and Sid both knew being close to their daughter meant they would leave all the pleasures they enjoyed in Las Vegas. They knew Ohio was ***not*** a good idea. Shirley was overbearing and controlling. As lovely and loving as she was at times, she was not an easy person to be close to. At the risk of disappointing her, they rejected Ohio.

Sid and Enid made it very clear to Shirley that they

wanted a loving relationship with her. They explained that they were saying ***NO*** to Ohio and not to her. Enid reassured her daughter that they would buy an assisted living apartment with an extra room so she could visit often. They are settling in with the help of friends and the fun of continuing all of their favorite lifestyles. Their meals are served and the housekeeping is done. They have their own furniture and beloved belongings. They have each other. Sid told me his huge sigh of relief could be heard all the way to Ohio. He said, "It is difficult to admit how difficult our daughter is, but I thank God every day we're not in Ohio." They truly don't need or want any kudos or validation. They are very pleased with their decision and proud of themselves.

ONE MISTAKE AFTER ANOTHER

Sid and Enid met Karen. She has an apartment in the same assisted living development. Karen defines the problem of not saying ***NO***. She told Enid that she lived in Arizona before she moved to Las Vegas to be with her daughter Pauline. Pauline insisted that Karen move to Las Vegas to live with her. Pauline sold Karen's car and house in Arizona. She signed Karen's name to all the necessary paperwork. Karen was stunned that Pauline would do this. Pauline explained they would use the money to live more comfortably together. When Karen objected, Pauline replied, "It's over. There's nothing you can do about it unless you want to put me in jail." Karen was certainly not inclined to put her daughter in jail, even though she deserved it.

Karen felt reluctant to hurt Pauline despite her illegal and dismissive behavior. Having no other choice, Karen settled down, determined to accept the situation.

She concentrated on the positives. Pauline had a nice home. They had a swimming pool and nice neighbors. Karen was becoming acclimated to this situation when another shoe dropped. Pauline got married. The honeymooning couple needed to have privacy. They couldn't have a normal married life if they were burdened with a mother-in-law. Before she knew what was happening, Karen was moved. She is now living in a one-bedroom apartment in an assisted living facility. She now lives in the same senior facility that Enid lives in. They have become friends. They share what almost happened to Enid, and what did happen to Karen. A definitive ***NO*** would have been a better choice for Karen as it was for Enid. Karen often wishes she were back in Arizona. Enid is thrilled she's not in Ohio.

"You cannot make the same mistake twice. The second time it's a choice."

– Anonymous

If you are faced with a decision, use the information in this book. You have the information you need to avoid such tragedies. Remember, that I foolishly would not sue my relative for the money he owed me. I know it is very difficult to hurt a loved one, even when it means protecting yourself. We all need to be totally determined to protect ourselves regardless of any emotional component.

GREED, LIES AND BETRAYAL

There is one man who belongs in jail. He stripped his wife of every luxury before leaving her for another woman. He twisted his wife's loyalty by telling her they were having financial problems. After 55 years of marriage, Henry told Gloria their business was failing. He told her she had to sell her jewelry to bail their family out of debt. She did sell her jewelry and gave Herman the money. She actually apologized, saying she kept her wedding ring. A few months later, he announced that he was selling their fabulous waterfront home in Hewlett Harbor. Gloria again signed all the necessary sale papers because she believed Herman. They moved into a smaller house in Cedarhurst. Gloria felt very proud that she was able to help their family and solve their financial problems. Exactly three weeks after they'd moved, Henry left home and told Gloria to file for divorce.

Gloria had access to the financial papers of the

business. She knew how much money was in the bank and what business contracts were paid monthly. She had all of the information at her fingertips. If she'd looked, she'd have seen a thriving business. She'd have uncovered the truth that there was no loss of income and no reason to sell anything. She would still have her jewelry and her beautiful home. If they did divorce, she'd still own half of the mansion they had sold. She would not feel so foolish and naïve. She could have protected herself and been proud of it. She could have said ***NO***.

Instead, she lived in a two bedroom house on a busy street. She had no claim to the yacht docked at her waterfront home. She had no profits from the sales they had made and she was divorced. She could have said ***NO*** to all of it. Learn from this and others like it. Get the facts. Ask questions. Be self-protective. Ask yourself, what is **BEST** for me at this moment? Loving someone does not mean they love you or that they are fair and honest. Be careful. Remember to ask, ***wha***t ***is good for me at this moment?***

Information and self-confidence will save you from bad decisions. Be prepared because your reactions are vulnerable without a plan. It's difficult to think so quickly. The persuasive techniques people used to get what they want are like a tsunami, drowning your confidence. Loving relationships and happy memories get in the way of logic. The questions thrown at you are often manipulative and confusing. This book ***"YOU***

COULD'VE SAID NO" gives you the ammunition, information and tools to decide in your own favor.

Have you ever behaved destructively? Have you ever allowed your trust and innocence to thrust you into a nightmare? With the knowledge you've gained, are you more aware of events that could happen? Are you now more wary, more careful and more in charge of your decisions? Are you holding on to the word ***NO***, in case you need it?

I, myself, was not immune to these dangers. A very close relative was losing his business. Fortunately, I was financially able to help. I gave him a great deal of money. He insisted on giving me a contract detailing collateral and interest promised. I reassured him that I didn't want money to be an issue. Our relationship soured from the very moment he cashed my checks. Was he guilty that he'd taken so much money? Did he feel ashamed of needing my help? Whatever the cause, he began to distance himself. Today we are completely estranged. Contact is barely polite and very rare. I never mention the money. I did destroy the contract and told him that I'd never consider a lawsuit. However, our relationship has never been as it was. In fact, we are basically alienated. What mistakes did I make?

In hindsight, I know that I should not have lent such a large amount. I also now know that it would have been advisable to begin a lawsuit. I used the defensive statement

"I'm not that kind of person." These words are merely a crutch to stand on when you're too weak to move forwards on your own behalf. I share this issue to illustrate we're all vulnerable. We need personal strength and tools to help. We need to say ***NO*** before we endure the pain that ensues from such mistakes.

There are endless examples of betrayed people. Too many others are greedy and determined to get what they want, regardless of the pain it causes. These immoral men and women are blind to the needs of their victims. They have no empathy or sensitivity to the results of their manipulations. Even more sadly, many don't care and they usually take no action to mitigate the destruction they've caused. It is difficult to believe that children can be rightfully described with these words. It is impossible to imagine a child being so manipulative and self-serving towards anyone, especially their parent. They are. Some are without conscience or sensitivity. They want what they want without concern for anyone. They are ruthless. You have to be on guard. If you are facing any problem with your adult child, do NOT be misled. Be strong and self-loving. Be true to yourself. Protect what you have. Protect yourself. Say ***NO***.

PANDEMIC DIARY
Day 128
July 18, 2020

INTENTIONS

"Intention is essential for success."
– Carole Altman

Wayne Dyer is the author of "PULLING YOUR OWN STRINGS" is based on the principles of self-protection. Dr. Dyer followed his own advice when his book was rejected by many publishers. He painted his van brightly with his title and he drove from college to university to major offices. He offered to give a speech to any group who would listen. He sold books from the back of his van. He has now written 20 bestsellers. He pulled himself up by his own bootstraps. His message is simple. Don't abuse yourself and don't allow abuse from anyone else. Nothing is impossible unless you don't even try.

His main premise is INTENTION. His intention was to have his book published and since no publisher was willing, he did it himself. The concept is that we all have the ability to accomplish and achieve.

IF YOU PERCEIVE IT YOU CAN ACHIEVE IT. Of course, I'm not suggesting we all publish a book. I am suggesting you can decide on what it is you want and go for it.

Write a list of your hopes and dreams. Then make your list of INTENTIONS. Here are six choices for you to aspire to:

<u>More self-control:</u> I intend to evaluate each possibility and always seek benefit TO ME.

<u>Self-love:</u> I intend to give to those I love. I intend to Give MORE love to those who love ME and always have enough love for MYSELF.

<u>The ability to relax:</u> I intend to learn the miraculous and effective techniques of relaxing which are available.

<u>More happiness:</u> I intend to choose happiness (it is available if you look). Removing the weeds reveals the flowers.

<u>Better health:</u> I intend to research my physical issues and improve them.

<u>Better social life:</u> I intend to make plans, seek friends, join groups, etc.

I think I said enough. It's all been said and written and sung. It's up to you. You are the author of your script. The buck stops with YOU.

Take a broom and sweep away the garbage that's weighing you down. No one can do it for you. Remember that those around you wish you would. You are a better person and a better friend when you are independent and self-reliant. It is so much more admirable to be evolved and dependable, than it is to be needy and weak.

"Love is the energy of life."

DECISION-MAKING NEEDS STYLE

"Always make decisions that prioritize your inner peace." – Anonymous

Take a moment now and reflect on how you respond to the requests of your loved ones? Reflect on the validity of the request. Evaluate who wants something from you. What needs are they asking you to satisfy? Is there consideration for your needs? Recognize who you are and what are the lifelong belief systems you hold. Look at your history as a decision maker. Have you been self-reliant, self-protective, wise? Have you been spontaneous, easy and unaware of the ramifications of your decisions? If you ask yourself, ***what is good for me at this moment***, it will help your decision. Have you ever asked this all-important question? Do you even consider yourself when a loved one is involved?

It is difficult to decide what is best for YOU when a

request is made? Why do we continue to create excuses to allow others to abuse us? Are we blind to the truth that many requests are abusive? Do we deny that someone we love and trust is capable of wanting more than we should give? Do they ask what they know is not best for us? Can they be that selfish? Yes, they can, and you have read many sad situations which could and should have been avoided. All of these stories will remind you to ask ***what's best for me at this moment.***

What is your style of decision making? Hopefully you will utilize all of these, carefully studying the situation and slowly deciding. Remember the mantra ***what is best for me at this moment***? Use every one of these styles:

Directive: Concern with results and creative approaches to the situation

Analytic: Concern with solid data. Just the facts and nothing else.

Behavioral: Concern with absolutes and low tolerance for ambiguity.

Too often, our fears and anxieties drive us into truly horrible situations. It is especially difficult to believe that a loved one is asking something of you that is NOT BEST for you. After all, how can we believe a daughter does not truly believe you should live with her? Can a loving son expect you to leave your home and friends because it's better for you? These scenarios are not only possible, but they are often played out in real time. The message is, we must not look back on any mistake or misjudgments. We must look forward to the future and the value of the information in this book. You don't have to regret anything. You can always say the self-protectivc ***NO.***

THE VALUES

These are not uncommon stories. These are the stories that are buried by feelings of humiliation and pain. How many of us are willing to share stories about the cruelty we suffered at the hands of our children? How many can share the pain inflicted by their own flesh and blood? In my case, I learned that secrets are kept because of the destructive emotion called shame. I also know that shame is a poison that creates disease, negative emotions and withdrawal.

My purpose in sharing these stories is to prevent the pain suffered by too many people. I concentrated on personal stories because I knew the victims as they struggled out of the hell that they created for themselves. Their sense of guilt and shame was crushing. Some were clients, some were family and some were friends. They all agreed to share anonymously.

I offer information which enables you to use these tools to avoid suffering. Making the right decision guarantees you will avoid the pain. Becoming aware of your emotional limitations enables you to avoid making an emotionally charged mistake. I know how negative treatment in your childhood can be debilitating and cause permanent damage. If you have memories of mistreatment that haunt you, I hope you can benefit from this information. I hope that by describing some of these factors, you will be enabled to face your demons and destroy them.

I shared my own demons and how I fought back and won. Again, the information is shared in the hopes it will lead you to victory. Ask the questions, use all the information available to you and make decisions which favor YOU. If you are faced with a request that is not positive, you now have tools to fight. You also now know that you are entitled to say ***NO.***

I want a life of health and happiness. I refuse to feel the poison of shame. Secrets are infused into our psyche by shame. Secrets are the fuel of shame. Too many of us have been victimized by destructive requests. Too many have been victimized because they allowed it. Taking responsibility, learning from it and moving on is essential. My life has been strewn with mistakes, sadness and failures. None of these horrors is a secret. Contrarily, I also talk about my successes and honors without embarrassment. All of who I am is in the light. I am the sum total of **ALL** of my experiences, as are you. If I am judged negatively, I accept the judgment. I do NOT allow it to be a burden. If I am rejected or disliked for valid reasons, I attempt to make changes. Fecling this level of confidence gives me the ability to say ***NO*** regardless of what might ensue. Saying ***NO i***s not a crime. It is not negative or cruel or dismissive behavior. It is an essential power that is not used effectively or often enough. Yes is often easier. ***NO*** is more difficult. But, remember that ***NO*** is protective and decisive. Use it wisely and avoid tragedy.

Let's examine a pertinent aspect of the psychology of ***NO***. Some of our childhood memories of the word ***NO*** are painful and oppressive. Our brain has become hardwired to resist these emotional memories by avoiding the word ***NO***. We are actually battling a physiological demon when we are faced with needing to reject an idea or behavior. Luckily, our brain is also logical, thoughtful and is our own best weapon for survival. The techniques and skills in this book reflect the power and fuel of logic. It is always productive and positive when you have a plan with effective tools in your quiver. ***"YOU COULD'VE SAID NO"*** is your survival plan.

Protect your attitude and well-being. Keep yourself positive and kind. Whatever the results, be free of shame and the ancillary diseases accompanied by shame. Think about what you are suffering because of secrets. Think about the help you can give others by sharing your mistakes. Most importantly, think about your own health.

DECISION-MAKING 101

"Being liked by others is a by-product of saying yes. Liking yourself sometimes comes only from saying NO."

– Anonymous

Rules governing decision-making.

1. What decision is BEST FOR ME?
2. Who is asking and what are they asking?
3. How do I feel about this person?
4. Can my feelings influence me?
5. Can I avoid the emotional pressures?
6. How will my life change?
7. What is the motivation for this request?
8. Is this request considering my needs?
9. Is this decision positive for happiness for BOTH of us?
10. How long has this been an issue?
11. How do others feel about this request?

12. Will I be giving up anything?
13. What past experiences do I have to help make this decision?
14. What is your history with the person requesting?

Being skilled in making decisions is essential for all of us. Choosing between two alternatives is commonplace. What should we eat? Where should we go? Should I buy this suit or that suit? There are many easy decisions. What about all the hard ones? Are you careful? Do you study the facts? Do you weigh all the possibilities? Do you protect yourselves? I'm sure in most instances most people don't even consider they ought to be self-protective when making decisions. However, there are some situations which require intense and intelligent processes. Agreeing to a change in your life, however simple or easy, is certainly one of these situations.

WHAT IF?

What if Ilene had asked these questions of her son, Josh? What if Liz had seen the reality of Roger's avarice and lack of consideration or love? What if Madge had said ***NO***? What if Gloria refused Henry's request? What if she'd armed herself with the knowledge that there was no financial problem? In every situation, the lack of knowledge was most damaging. Asking questions will protect you as these victims could have protected themselves.

Sadly, seniors are especially vulnerable. We have given our children everything. We wanted them to have a better life than we did. Too many of the now adult men and women are convinced that we will continue to give them everything. These young adults feel empowered to ask, for and they feel entitled to get. We, the loving parents, are faced with outrageous requests based on our past behavior. Too many young adults are irresponsible, selfish and incredibly demanding. Too many parents behave under the guise of love by giving, *giving* and then ***giving*** even more. This is a serious phenomenon which seems to be terribly prevalent. This is a detailed warning for all of us since it has happened to many others who fail to be self-protective. Beware of the false and unjustly labeled ***needs*** and the cries for so-called ***essentials.***

What if we all embraced this and acted upon it?

"Kindness is the beauty that the blind can see and the deaf can hear." – Anonymous

What if we begin to demand that these adults take responsibility and earn what they need and what they feel is essential to their lives. Earn it yourself is a good answer when faced with requests for something. Just before you say ***"NO,"*** give them a hug and a Help Wanted list. The saga of the millennials is pressing on us as we become a sandwich generation. What if we refuse to accept the role? What if we remember we are in charge?

"YOU COULD'VE SAID NO" is your encyclopedia for protective and intelligent decision making. When faced with a conflict, examine these pages. See the truth behind the question. Examine the motivation and reality of the request. See your own truth of what you need and really want. Trust your instincts. Depend on the facts. Do everything you can to see the danger of emotional tugs and manipulative promises. If emotion is involved, the brain becomes paralyzed. Wake up your right brain and give yourself time to think and remember to ask ***what is best for me at this moment?***

Yes is too often a cause of pain and a thief of time. Love is a self-loving positive choice and a safe conclusion.

Win a personal award for decision-making skills. Earn 100% in this class of DECISION-MAKING 101. Happiness is a choice which is YOURS to make.

"Love is the energy of life."
– Carole Altman

ABOUT THE AUTHOR

Dr. Carole Altman is a therapist and an award-winning author for her book, "You Can Be Your Own Sex Therapist." Her career spans 60+ years, including giving lectures and workshops teaching the art of happy, positive living.

She is determined to share pertinent skills and information which are necessary in the quest for emotional and spiritual success.

Dr. Altman has been a guest on many television shows, including her own, "Awareness with Carole Altman" in New York City.

Her approach is down-to-earth, effective and practical, following the founder of Gestalt Therapy, Dr. Fritz Perls.

Dr. Altman is a pioneer in the Human Potential Movement, working as President of Aueron, Esalen East. She developed systems in therapy which build confidence and nurture personal power. Her process concentrates on natural behaviors leading to enhancement of your confidence and pride. This book offers the information and the emotional strength to take control of every aspect of your life, including the necessity of saying ***NO***.

Carole believes that life is a rainbow, removing the weed reveals the flower and love is the energy of life.

Dr. Altman has published several books and is especially proud of ***"YOU COULD'VE SAID NO: SELF-LOVING DECISIONS ENHANCE YOUR QUALITY OF LIFE."***

www.ingramcontent.com/pod-product-compliance
Lightning Source LLC
LaVergne TN
LVHW050602160826
845677LV00011B/2429

* 9 7 9 8 6 6 9 5 0 0 0 6 1 *